Stranger Safety

by Lisa M. Herrington

Content Consultant
Debra Holtzman, J.D., M.A.

Reading Consultant
Jeanne Clidas, Ph.D.
Reading Specialist

Children's Press®
An Imprint of Scholastic Inc.
New York Toronto London Auckland Sydney
Mexico City New Delhi Hong Kong
Danbury, Connecticut

Dear Parent/Educator:
It is very important that children learn about stranger danger. However, this is something they might need help with from a grown-up. If your child needs that help, we hope you will use this book as a springboard to a discussion with him or her. You can read the book together the first time, and talk about the different suggestions inside. Make sure your child understands that behavior that would normally be considered unacceptable—such as kicking, biting, and fibbing—is acceptable, even advisable, when dealing with strangers.

Library of Congress Cataloging-in-Publication Data
Herrington, Lisa M.
Stranger safety / by Lisa M. Herrington.
 p. cm. — (Rookie read-about safety)
 Includes index.
 ISBN 978-0-531-28972-3 (library binding) — ISBN 978-0-531-29274-7 (pbk.)
 1. Children and strangers—Juvenile literature. 2. Safety education—Juvenile literature. 3. Crime prevention—Juvenile literature. I. Title.
 HQ784.S8H47 2013
 363.1'06—dc23   2012013378

Produced by Spooky Cheetah Press

1 2 3 4 5 6 7 8 9 10 R 22 21 20 19 18 17 16 15 14 13

Photographs © 2013: age fotostock/Barrie Fanton: 20; Alamy Images/Steve Skjold: 3, 27 inset; Getty Images: 19 (Altrendo Images), 12, 13, 16 (Robert E. Daemmrich); Keith Plechaty: cover; Media Bakery: 7 (Antenna), 28 (Charlie Schuck), 8 (Erik Isakson); PhotoEdit/Eric Fowke: 27 background; Thinkstock: 4, 31 top right (iStockphoto), 22, 23, 24, 25 (Jupiterimages/Getty Images), 31 bottom right (Siri Stafford), 11, 15, 31 bottom left, 31 top left.

Table of Contents

Safe Place

Who Are Strangers?

A stranger is a person you do not know. Most strangers will not hurt you, but you must be careful.

A stranger can seem nice, but do not talk to strangers, even if they know your name.

Stick with People You Know

Stay in groups with people you know. Do not go off by yourself.

Always stay with an adult or a buddy. Never go anywhere with a stranger.

Never get in a stranger's car. If a stranger stops, RUN and tell a grown-up you know.

Scream for help if a stranger tries to grab you. You can kick, scratch, or bite to free yourself. Run away as fast as you can.

Lies and Tricks

Sometimes strangers lie to you. They might say your family asked them to pick you up. Do not believe them. Your family would never send a stranger to get you.

Strangers may try to trick you. They might offer you toys or candy. Say no! Never take anything from a stranger.

A stranger might pretend to need help with a pet. Stay away! Remember: A grown-up you do not know should never ask you for help.

Stay Safe at Home

If you are home alone, never open the door for anyone. Dial 911 if you need help.

Never agree to meet someone you know only from the Internet. If a stranger contacts you, tell an adult.

If You Need Help...

If you are lost or need help, look for a "Safe Place." This might be a library, fire station, or YMCA. If you see a "Safe Place" sign, it is a good place to ask for help.

A police officer is a good person to ask for help. You can also ask a mom who has kids with her. Talk to a grown-up you trust about other adults you can ask for help.

Try It! Read the tip on this page again. With your parents or caregivers, make a list of people you can go to if you are lost or need help.

I Can Be Safe!

- Do not talk to strangers.

- Never go anywhere with a stranger.

- Never get in a stranger's car.

- Do not take anything from strangers.

- Ask a grown-up you trust to help you make a list of safe places where you can go for help.

Words You Know

car

fire station

pet

police officer

Index

Facts for Now

Visit this Scholastic Web site for more information on stranger safety:
www.factsfornow.scholastic.com
Enter the keyword **Stranger**

About the Author

Lisa M. Herrington writes print and digital materials for kids, teachers, and parents. She lives in Connecticut with her husband and daughter. She hopes all kids stay safe!